Gold Medal Advisory Board

OLYMPIC SPEED SKATING

By the staff of the Ice Skating Institute of America
in cooperation with the United States Olympic Committee

CP CHILDRENS PRESS, CHICAGO

The great Klas Thunberg of Finland won gold medals in 1924 and 1928. He also set records in three different events.

Photographs in this book courtesy of the Ice Skating Institute of America, publisher, *XIII Olympic Winter Games, Lake Placid,* © 1979. Created by T. A. Chacharon & Assoc. Ltd.

Cover photograph: Eric Heiden of the United States.
Page 1 photograph: Roald Aas of Norway won the gold medal in 1960.

LIBRARY OF CONGRESS CATALOGING IN PUBLICATION DATA

Ice Skating Institute of America.
  Olympic speed skating.

  SUMMARY: Presents accounts of Olympic speed skating competition beginning in 1924.
  1. Speed skating — History — Juvenile literature. 2. Speed skating — Records — Juvenile literature. 3. Olympic games (winter) — Records — Juvenile literature. [1. Speed skating — History. 2. Olympic games (winter) — History. 3. Speed skating — Records] I. United States Olympic Committee. II. Title.
GV850.3.I23   1979   796.9'1   79-16969
ISBN 0-516-02556-2

The day is cold and clear and sunny. The crowd murmurs as you glide to your position. The ice is hard and smooth—just perfect, you tell yourself.

You are just behind the starting line. The day is suddenly quiet; the sun is a spotlight; and your whole world is the sheet of ice in front of you. Your body is poised and ready. Your breathing is strong and confident. Your feet want to fly.

The starting gun sounds! You leap forward. The wind tears at your face. Your body is low to the ground, moving to a rhythm and a speed you've never felt before. You are flying! You rush around and around the track. There is nothing in your world except wind and skates and speed.

Ahead is the finish line. Now is the time to reach for that extra burst of energy. You give it your all. Go! Fly! The line passes under you. You've done it! You've skated faster than anyone else has ever skated before. The crowd roars its approval. You are the fastest skater in the whole world!

That is the dream and the hope of every contender who participates in the Olympic speed-skating competition. It is no wonder that this event is one of the most exciting and popular of the Olympic Winter Games.

5

*This drawing, done at the time, shows
Joseph F. Donoghue of the United States
beating the Russian Flyer, Alex von Panschin,
in the two-mile International Race
at Amsterdam on January 10, 1889.*

HOW SPEED SKATING STARTED

Competition has always been an important part of games and sports. It is natural for anyone engaging in a sport to want to be better or faster than anyone else. Skaters, for instance, have been racing each other for as long as people have been skating. Local contests for racing on skates developed very early, and then countries held national championships for skaters.

Finally, speed skating became the first winter sport to become an international event. The first world championship (for men) was held in 1889 in Amsterdam. When the International Skating Union (ISU) was formed in 1892, it took over the regulation of these championships. Speed skating for men was added to the first Winter Olympic Games of 1924.

A world championship for women was not held until 1936. Women's speed skating did not become an Olympic event until 1960.

SKATES AND SKATING TECHNIQUES

The skate used for speed skating has a straight blade, twelve to eighteen inches long. The blade is very thin, only $\frac{1}{32}''$ to $\frac{1}{16}''$ wide. This thin blade is set into a steel tube to make it stronger. The boot of the skate looks much like a shoe. It is low cut and made of very thin leather, with some reinforcement around the heel. The whole skate is very light in weight; this makes it easier for the skaters to move their feet quickly.

In making this speed-skating turn, the left shoulder is back and leaning into the turn. As the right leg begins the crossover, the right arm swings back and the left arm swings forward.

This skater is continuing a turn by pushing off the outside edge of the left skate. The right leg has crossed over, ready to begin the next stroke.

When coming out of the turn, the skater is ready to begin the straightaway stroke. As the left leg comes forward, the right arm swings forward and the left arm swings back.

Speed skating is usually done with a rolling motion. The skater uses one foot for pushing and the other foot for gliding. The push is done with the inside edge of the blade. During the push, the gliding blade is rolled from the outside edge to the inside edge. On the next stroke, it becomes the pushing skate.

Speed skaters keep their knees slightly bent. This enables them to perform the greatest amount of push. The skaters also bend forward at the waist to increase forward motion. In a short-distance race, skaters use only the forward part of the blade for the most speed. They swing their arms to give more power to the push. In longer distances, the skaters use more of the skate blade surface. To conserve energy, one arm may be swung or the hands may be clasped behind the back.

Skaters wear lightweight, warm clothing for a race, since speed skating is an outdoor event. The outfits are fairly tight so they will not catch the wind and slow the skaters down. Skaters also wear safety helmets. Some skaters go as fast as thirty miles per hour when they are racing, and could hurt themselves if they fell.

9

*A speed-skating
starting position*

*Front view of a
speed-skating crossover.*

*Side view
of a
speed-skating
crossover.*

TRAINING FOR THE OLYMPICS

Skaters are trained differently in the United States than they are in Europe. United States speed skating is done *pack-style.* This means that several skaters race at a time instead of just two. The skaters race against each other instead of against the clock. Several rounds, or *heats,* are held. The winners of each heat compete in a semi-final heat, and then a final race to see who the winner is.

Skaters start out in "dry training." They do not start on ice. They jog, stretch, and practice skating positions. They get into shape. The stronger their bodies are, the less chance they have of getting hurt.

Finally the skaters move to the ice. They start out on an indoor ice rink, which is not as large as an outdoor track. They are taught how to "stroke" with their skates. They practice ways to start a race. They work to increase their speed. They start holding races. Their coaches watch them and take pictures and movies to help the skaters learn where they are making mistakes.

When outside temperatures are low enough to keep ice frozen, the skaters work on the outdoor track. They are divided by age and ability into five divisions. Midget division skaters are ten and eleven years old. The Juvenile division skaters are twelve and thirteen years old. Intermediate skaters are sixteen and seventeen, and Senior skaters are eighteen years or older. Skaters may compete in higher divisions, but may not compete with skaters younger than themselves. Each division participates in races that are held all over the United States. The best skaters in these races switch to *metric-style,* or Olympic, speed skating.

11

*Indoor skaters
practice their start.*

*After the start,
skaters spread out.*

*In long races, skaters are
lined up, one behind another.*

These skaters compete in regional, national, and international speed-skating meets. Those who do well are invited by the United States Olympic committee to compete in selection trials. From these races the very best skaters are chosen for the United States Olympic speed-skating team.

13

Muratov Valeriy of the U.S.S.R.
skates his way to a silver
medal at Innsbruck, Austria in 1976.

400 METER TRACK

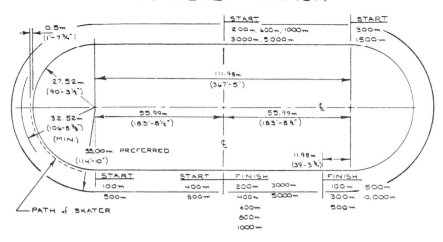

OLYMPIC COMPETITION

Olympic speed skating is a race against the clock. Two skaters at a time race on a track that is 333⅓ to 400 meters long. The ice of the track is divided into two lanes.

Races of different length are skated. For men, the distances are 500, 1,500, 5,000, and 10,000 meters. In addition, at the 1976 Olympics a 1,000-meter event was added. For women the races are 500, 1,000, 500, and 3,000 meters long. Medals are awarded separately for each race. Each country may enter teams of twelve men and eight women.

In an Olympic speed-skating race, the two skaters for each race draw for lanes. One will start on the inside lane and one will start on the outside. The skaters change lanes with every lap of the track. This is because the inner lane is a shorter distance around and each skater must skate the same distance.

A score is determined by the time it takes each skater to finish the race. Time is figured down to hundredths of seconds. The skater with the lowest time in each event is the winner. In case of a tie, two medals are awarded.

15

THE BEST SPEED SKATERS IN THE WORLD

Olympic speed-skating events have always been exciting. The international spirit of the competition is clear. The skaters are racing against a common enemy—time. Second by second, they whittle away at time records. They pit their skills, training, and willpower against the limits of their bodies. Each skater wants to be perfect—the best. Because of this, the skaters win or lose against themselves and against time. The race toward perfection, the race to beat the clock, provides the drama of the games. The players and the settings for this drama make Olympic history.

Let's look at some of the record-breaking skaters who have competed in the Olympics.

MEN In the first Winter Olympics in 1924 medals were awarded in each of the four races. In addition, that year a gold medal was awarded to an overall winner. This was the only Olympics in which this medal was awarded. The overall winner, who had to win three of the four races, was **Clas Thunberg** of Finland. He and Norwegian skater **Ivar Ballangrud** were probably the greatest all-round masters of speed skating. After that first winter Olympics, speed skaters began to specialize in one or two events rather than in overall competiton.

17

Irving Jaffee of the United States won his third gold medal in 1932 by diving across the finish line. A few years later Jaffee sold all his medals in order to support his family.

Each country seemed to be strongest in a certain event. The speed-skating sprint (500 meters) suited United States skaters. The 1924 gold medal for this distance was won by **Charles Jewtraw.** In later Olympics, **John Shea** in 1932 and **Kenneth Henry** in 1952, also from the United States, won gold medals. Through the 1960 Olympics, American skaters also brought home four silver and two bronze medals in the 500-meter event.

In the 1,500-meter event, Norway and Finland had many Olympic medalists through 1960. **Clas Thunberg** won this race in 1924 and 1928. Skaters from the U.S.S.R. did well in the 1956 Olympics. One of the winners was **Eugeny Grischin,** the first 1,500-meter medalist from the U.S.S.R.

Until 1960, Norwegian skaters dominated the 5,000-meter event. They won four gold, two silver, and three bronze medals. This distance was the specialty of **Ivar Ballangrud.** He took the gold in 1928 and 1936. Skaters from the U.S.S.R. were also strong in this event in 1956, when they brought in their first gold medal.

A look at the 10,000-meter event through 1960 shows that Sweden, Norway, and Finland produced most of the winning skaters. **Irving Jaffee** of the United States won a gold medal in the 1932 competition, and the U.S.S.R. took home a bronze medal in 1956.

Squaw Valley, California, 1960 The design for the Squaw Valley Olympic site was very different from that of previous Olympic sites. Distances between the various events were quite short. This made it possible for spectators to walk across the hard-packed snow from one contest to another in just a few minutes. The Americans also had planned the best possible skating conditions. They had built the first

*Kenneth Henry of the United States
enters a turn on his way to victory
at the Oslo, Norway Olympics of 1952.*

*Left to right, the 1,500-meter 1952
medal winners: Roald Aas of Norway (bronze),
Willem van de Voort of the Netherlands (silver),
and Hjalmar Andersen of Norway (gold).*

artificial speed-skating rink in the world. For the first time, competitors did not have to depend on the weather for good ice.

Even with these nearly perfect conditions, however, hopes were not high for the speed-skating events in 1960. The 1956 Olympic skaters had set records that many people felt could not be broken. They were proved right—except for one event.

In the 500-meter race **Eugeny Grishin** just missed breaking the 40-second mark. He won another gold medal in this event, tying his own Olympic record of 40.2 seconds. Seven other skaters also succeeded in covering the 500 meters in less than 41 seconds. American **William Disney** took second place in that race. His speed was one-tenth of a second slower than Grishin's.

21

Left to right, the 500-meter 1952 medal winners: Don McDermott of the United States (silver), Kenneth Henry of the United States (gold), Gordon Audley of Canada (bronze), and Arne Johansen of Norway (bronze).

Roald Aas of Norway races through a heavy snowstorm.

The next day the 5,000-meter event was held. **Victor Koskichkin's** accomplishments for the U.S.S.R. were outstanding. He won with a time of 7:51.3. Even so, he was a full three seconds behind countryman **Boris Schilkow,** the 1956 winner.

There were strong winds on the next day. The skaters in the 1,500-meter race were bothered by them. **Roald Aas** of Norway overcame that problem, however, and tied **Grishin** of the U.S.S.R. for first place. They both received a gold medal.

In the 1,000-meter event on the last day of competition, **Knut Johannesen** of Norway smashed previous Olympic records with his time of 15:46.6. He had beaten the 1956 winner's time by an incredible 49.3 seconds!

*Opposite: Three medal winners
in the 1968 500-meter event
at Grenoble, France.
Left to right: Terry McDermott
of the United States (silver),
Erhard Keller of West Germany (gold),
and Magne Thomassen of Norway (silver).*

Innsbruck, Austria, 1964 **Terry McDermott** returned to the United States from Innsbruck with the only gold medal won by an American.

The 500-meter sprint is always exciting. The skaters race as fast and as hard as they can. The faster skaters usually prefer to skate early in the competition. The ice is better, and so is the competition.

McDermott, however, preferred to race against the clock. He asked his coach to place him later in the competition. He would know by then the time he had to beat. When he finally took his position, the best time was 40.6 seconds.

McDermott covered the distance in 40.1 seconds. It was a world's record, an Olympic record, and meant the only gold medal for the Americans at Innsbruck.

25

Grenoble, France, 1968   Among the many skaters who were entered in the 500-meter race at Grenoble were two gold medalists, **Terry McDermott** and **Eugeny Grishin.** Eleven other skaters in that race had recorded times under 41 seconds. It was not surprising that there was very strong competition for the medals.

Early in the race, West Germany's **Erhard Keller** made a time of 40.3 seconds. It proved to be unbeatable. Rising temperatures softened the ice and slowed down the later skaters.

McDermott skated last in the race. He had a tremendous opening burst, but the soft ice kept him from keeping the pace. He finished in 40.5 seconds to tie for second place.

The 5,000-meter race was next. **Fred Maier,** the world champion from Norway, saw his world record time of 7:26.2 bettered by **Kees Verkerk** of the Netherlands. That did not discourage Maier. Later in the day he beat Verkerk's new record by nine-tenths of a second—a new world's record and a gold medal speed.

Kees Verkerk found consolation in the next event. He won the 1,500-meter race. The silver medalist was **Ard Schenk,** also from the Netherlands. This gave Holland a total of four medals of a possible twelve for the speed-skating events.

27

*Opposite: Hjalmar Andersen
of Norway sets a new Olympic record
and wins his third gold medal in 1952.*

Finally it was time for the last event. The 10,000-meter race was skated in strong winds, which greatly bothered the skaters. The gold medal was won by Sweden's **Johnny Hoeglin. Fred Maier** took the silver for his second medal in the 1968 games.

Sapporo, Japan, 1972   The most exciting speed-skating event in Sapporo was the men's 500-meter sprint. For the first time, the 40-second barrier was broken in Olympic competition. West Germany's **Erhard Keller** took the gold medal, as he had in the 1968 Games. He skated the distance in 39.44 seconds. Only two-tenths of a second separated the top three skaters. All had times of less than 40 seconds.

In the 1,500-meter race, **Ard Schenk** from the Netherlands took the gold medal. He had taken a silver medal in the 1968 Olympics. In the 1972 Games, Schenk beat **Roar Gronvold** of Norway by 1.3 seconds.

In Schenk's next event, the 5,000-meter race, everything seemed to be going against him. He had to start first, and during his race it snowed heavily. But Schenk could not be denied victory. Again he won, forcing Gronvold to another second-place finish.

But Schenk was not through yet. In the 1,000-meter contest, he took his third gold medal of the 1972 Games. He beat **Kees Verkerk's** second-place time by only three seconds. Ard Schenk went home from Japan a very happy man.

29

*Opposite: Karla Guseva of the U.S.S.R.
speeds to a gold medal in the 1,000-meter
event at Squaw Valley, California in 1960.*

Innsbruck, Austria, 1976   A high point for the United States speed-skating team at Innsbruck was a brand-new event—the men's 1,000-meter race. **Peter Mueller,** who was engaged to United States speed skater Leah Poulos, won the gold medal. It was a happy day—the United States team's last gold medal for speed skating had been won by Terry McDermott in 1964.

The United States team was not satisfied with only one medal. In the 500-meter event, **Dan Immerfall** earned the bronze. He beat Sweden's **Matt Wallberg** by only *two one-hundredths* of a second.

The team from the Netherlands did even better than they had in 1972. They took five medals. The U.S.S.R. and Norwegian teams also made strong showings, each taking four medals.

Opposite: Peter Mueller of the United States, who won the gold in the 1976 1,000-meter race at Innsbruck, stands with his fiance Leah Poulos, who won a silver in the 1,000-meter race that same year.

WOMEN In 1932 speed-skating demonstrations by women were part of the Olympic program at Lake Placid, but no medals were awarded for them. In 1960, because of the efforts of the U.S.S.R., these competitions were finally given full Olympic status. Women's competitions are very popular in the U.S.S.R.

Only twenty-three women skaters from ten countries entered those first Olympic races. Even today, fewer women than men race in speed-skating competitions.

Squaw Valley, California, 1960 The Russian team was favored to win all the events at Squaw Valley. **Helga Haase** from Germany, however, surprised everyone by taking a gold medal in the first event, the 500-meter race. **Natalija Donchenko** of the U.S.S.R. took a silver and **Jeanne Ashworth** of the United States a bronze. Only three-tenths of a second separated all these skaters.

*Lidia Skoblikova of the U.S.S.R.
proudly shows the two gold medals
she won at Squaw Valley in 1960.
Four years later, at Innsbruck, Austria,
Skoblikova won all four
women's speed-skating events.*

The U.S.S.R. team did manage to win the next three events. In the 1,500-meter race, **Lidia Skoblikova** established a world-record time and took the gold medal. **Karla Guseva** claimed another victory for the U.S.S.R. in the 1,000-meter event. She beat Haase by two-tenths of a second. Lidia Skoblikova, with one gold medal already won, carried off the honors in the 3,000-meter race. Her teammate **Valentina Stenina** won the silver in the same event.

Innsbruck, Austria, 1964 At Innsbruck **Lidia Skoblikova** of the U.S.S.R. was the whole story in women's speed skating. She won *all four* events, and set Olympic records in three of them. Skoblikova broke records in the 500-meter, 1,000-meter, and 1,500-meter races. It was the first time that anyone, man or woman, had won four gold medals in the Winter Olympics.

Skoblikova worried after taking her first gold medal that she was being too greedy by entering all four events. A telephone call to her friends and family at home, however, convinced her that she should do the very best she could in all the races.

Perhaps her most impressive victory was in the 3,000-meter event, even though she did not set a new record. She was skating near the end of the event. The skaters who had raced before her had softened the ice. It is very hard to skate fast on soft ice. Skoblikova had to work twice as hard to win. Her coaches called out to her to slow down. But she gave her best in the race and was rewarded with another gold medal.

*Opposite: Dianne Holum of the United States,
a 1968 medalist, is coach of the 1980 United States team.*

Grenoble, France, 1968 The opening day of the speed-skating competitions in Grenoble was made very exciting by the strange events that took place during the 500-meter sprint race. United States skater **Mary Meyers,** at that time the world-champion speed skater, was the front-runner early in the competition. Her time was 46.3 seconds. Later in the event **Ludmila Titova** of the U.S.S.R. moved Meyers to second place with her time of 46.1 seconds. Though this turned out to be the winning time, the competition was not over yet.

In the race immediately following Titova's, **Dianne Holum** of the United States gave an all-out effort. Her time was 46.3, the same as Mary Meyers's time. In the final race, **Jennifer Fish,** also an American, added to the audience's amazement. Fish also clocked a time of 46.3 seconds. For the first time in Olympic history, three skaters from the same team had tied for an Olympic medal!

Sapporo, Japan, 1972 At Sapporo **Anne Henning** of the United States proved she was truly an Olympic champion. She won the gold medal for the 500-meter race—twice. Ann raced in the fifth pair with Canadian skater **Sylvia Burka.** As Anne changed lanes, Sylvia got in her way. Despite this, Anne broke the Olympic record with a time of 43.73 seconds. However, the coach of the United States team filed a protest, which was honored. So when the rest of the skaters had completed their races, Anne did another sprint over the 500-meters—this time alone. The clock showed an even better time of 43.33. Anne had beaten everyone, even herself!

37

Above: Dianne Holum won a gold medal for the 1,500-meter race in the 1972 Olympics at Sapporo. Opposite: Anne Henning of the United States won a gold for the 500-meter race in 1972.

Monika Pflug of West Germany was the gold-medal winner in the 1,000-meter race. **Anne Henning** took a bronze medal in this event, to add to her gold.

In the 1,500-meter race, **Dianne Holum** of the United States made her dream of winning a gold medal come true. In 1968 at Grenoble she had won silver and bronze medals. In Sapporo she skated a superb race and won a gold with her amazingly fast last lap.

The longest distance for the women—the 3,000-meter event—was a triumph for two Dutch skaters. **Stien Baas-Kaiser** was the top finisher, and **Atje Keulen-Deelstra** took her second bronze medal of the 1972 Games. **Dianne Holum,** with a tremendous effort, won the silver medal.

Innsbruck, Austria, 1976 For seven years the U.S.S.R. speed-skating ace, **Tatiana Averina,** had looked for victory in international competition. In the 500-meter event at Innsbruck she finished behind **Sheila Young** of the United States and **Cathy Priestner** of Canada.

Averina's moment of victory finally came in the running of the 1,000-meter race. She skated against three of the best speed skaters in the world: **Monika Holzner,** who had won this race in 1972, **Leah Poulos,** and **Sheila Young.** Leah Poulos came close to skating a perfect race. Her time of 1:28.57 put her in front of the other contenders. But Averina pulled ahead of Poulos in the very first lap. She won the gold medal with a time of 1:28.43. Poulos took the silver and Young the bronze. If the three skaters had raced side by side, there would have been only sixteen inches between the first, second, and third place winners.

Averina doubled her win by taking a second gold medal in the 3,000-meter race. **Sheila Young** ended up with one gold, one silver, and one bronze medal from the competition. It was truly a remarkable Olympic competition.

41

*Eric Heiden and his sister Beth are both
members of the 1980 United States Olympic team.*

Peter Mueller, a 1976 gold-medal winner,
is a member of the 1980 United States team.

*Leah Poulas Mueller,
member of the United States
Speed Skating Team.*

*Kim Kestrom, member of the
United States Speed Skating Team.*

Beth Heiden, member of
the United States Speed
Skating Team.

Scott Guy, member of the
World Sprint Speedskating Team.

Craig Kressler,
member of the World
Speedskating Team.

Dan Carroll, member of the World Speedskating Team.

Thomas Plant, member of the World Speedskating Team.

Michael Plant, member of the World Speedskating Team.

Olympic Gold Medalists
Speed Skating
Men

500 METERS

Year	Name	Country
1924	Charles Jewtraw	United States
1928	Clas Thunberg	Finland
1928	Bernt Evensen	Norway
1932	John A. Shea	United States
1936	Ivar Ballangrud	Norway
1948	Finn Helgesen	Norway
1952	Kenneth Henry	United States
1956	Yevgeni Grishin	U.S.S.R.
1960	Yevgeni Grishin	U.S.S.R.
1964	T. Richard McDermott	United States
1968	Erhard Keller	West Germany
1972	Erhard Keller	West Germany
1976	Evgeny Kulikov	U.S.S.R.

1000 METERS

Year	Name	Country
1976	Peter Mueller	United States

1500 METERS

Year	Name	Country
1924	Clas Thunberg	Finland
1928	Clas Thunberg	Finland
1932	John A. Shea	United States
1936	Charles Mathisen	Norway
1948	Sverre Farstad	Norway
1952	Hjalmar Andersen	Norway
1956	Yevgeni Grishin and Yuri Mikhailov	U.S.S.R.
1960	Yevgeni Grishin	U.S.S.R.
1960	Roald Aas	Norway
1964	Ants Antson	U.S.S.R.
1968	Cornelius Verkerk	Netherlands
1972	Ard Schenk	Netherlands
1976	Jan-Egil Storholt	Norway

5000 METERS

Year	Name	Country
1924	Clas Thunberg	Finland
1928	Ivar Ballangrud	Norway
1932	Irving Jaffee	United States
1936	Ivar Ballangrud	Norway
1948	Reidar Liaklev	Norway
1952	Hjalmar Andersen	Norway
1956	Boris Shilkov	U.S.S.R.
1960	Viktor Kositschkin	U.S.S.R.
1964	Knut Johannesen	Norway
1968	F. Anton Maier	Norway
1972	Ard Schenk	Netherlands
1976	Sten Stensen	Norway

10,000 METERS

Year	Name	Country
1924	Julius Skutnabb	Finland
1928	Irving Jaffee	United States
1932	Irving Jaffee	United States
1936	Ivar Ballangrud	Norway
1948	Ake Seyffarth	Sweden
1952	Hjalmar Andersen	Norway
1956	Sigvard Ericsson	Sweden
1960	Knut Johannesen	Norway
1964	Jonny Nilsson	Sweden
1968	Jonny Hoeglin	Sweden
1972	Ard Schenk	Netherlands
1976	Piet Kleine	Netherlands

Gold Medalists
Speed Skating
Women

	500 METERS			1000 METERS	
Year	**Name**	**Country**	**Year**	**Name**	**Country**
1960	Helga Haase	Germany	1960	Klara Guseva	U.S.S.R.
1964	Lidia Skoblikova	U.S.S.R.	1964	Lidia Skoblikova	U.S.S.R.
1968	Ludmila Titova	U.S.S.R.	1968	Carolina Geijssen	Netherlands
1972	Anne Henning	United States	1972	Monika Pflug	West Germany
1976	Sheila Young	United States	1976	Tatiana Averina	U.S.S.R.

	1500 METERS			3000 METERS	
Year	**Name**	**Country**	**Year**	**Name**	**Country**
1960	Lidia Skoblikova	U.S.S.R.	1960	Lidia Skoblikova	U.S.S.R.
1964	Lidia Skoblikova	U.S.S.R.	1964	Lidia Skoblikova	U.S.S.R.
1968	Kaija Mustonen	Finland	1968	Johanna Schut	Netherlands
1972	Dianne Holum	United States	1972	Stein Baas-Kaiser	Netherlands
1976	Galina Stepanskaya	U.S.S.R.	1976	Tatiana Averina	U.S.S.R.